Let's Go

written by Pam Holden

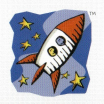

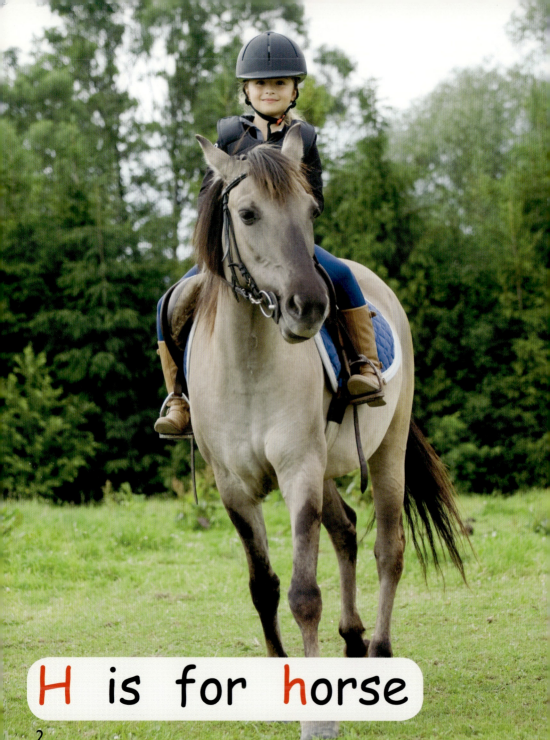

H is for horse

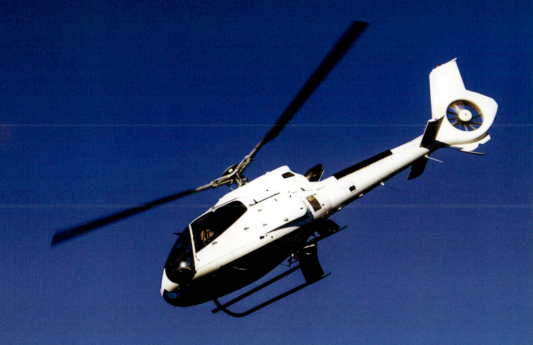

and h is for helicopter.

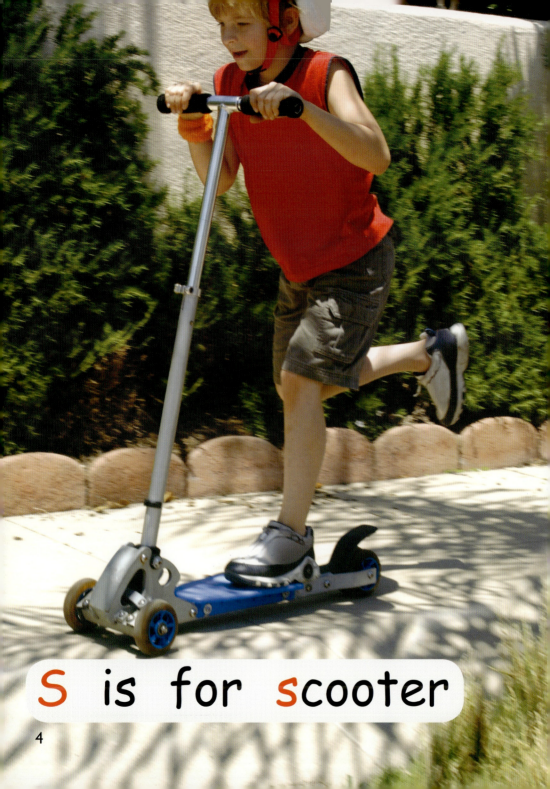

S is for scooter

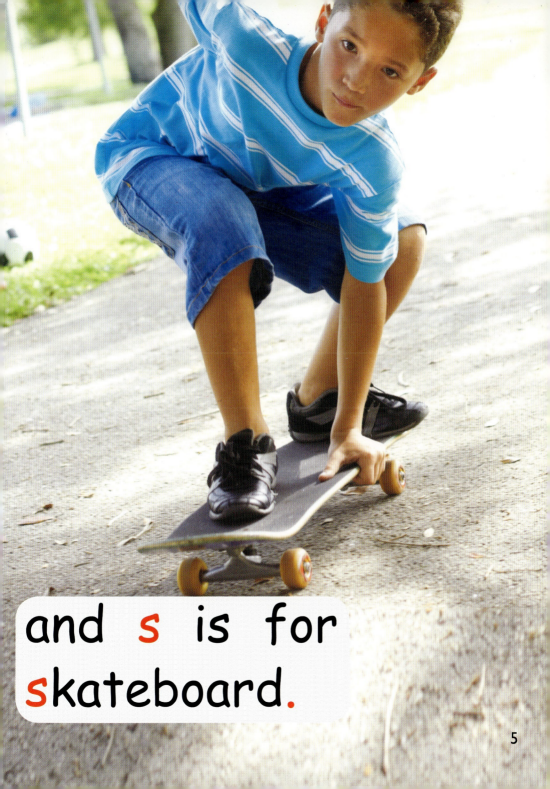

and s is for skateboard.

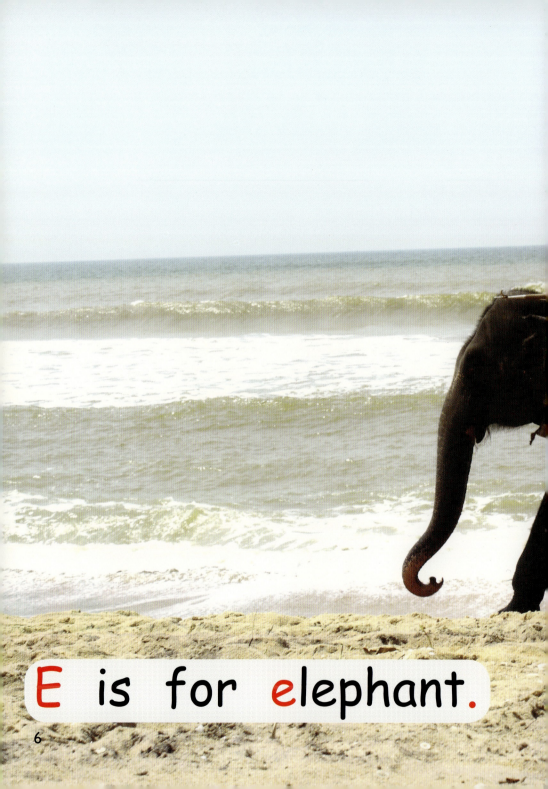
E is for elephant.

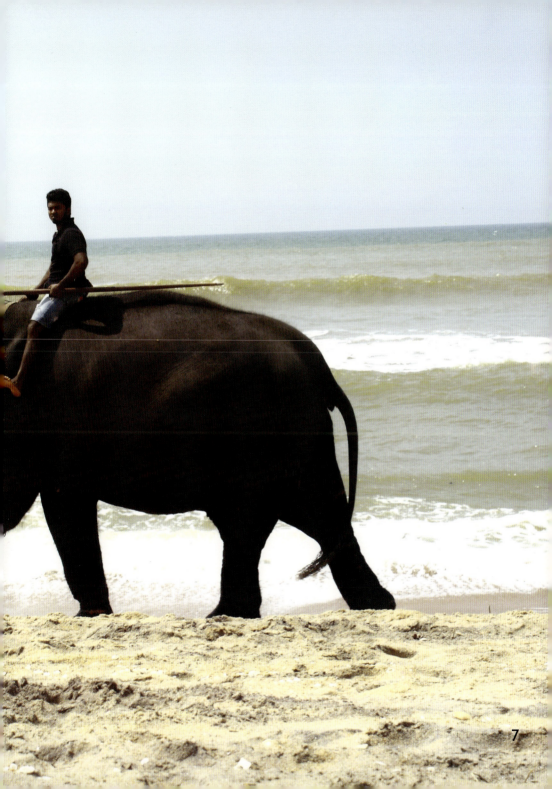

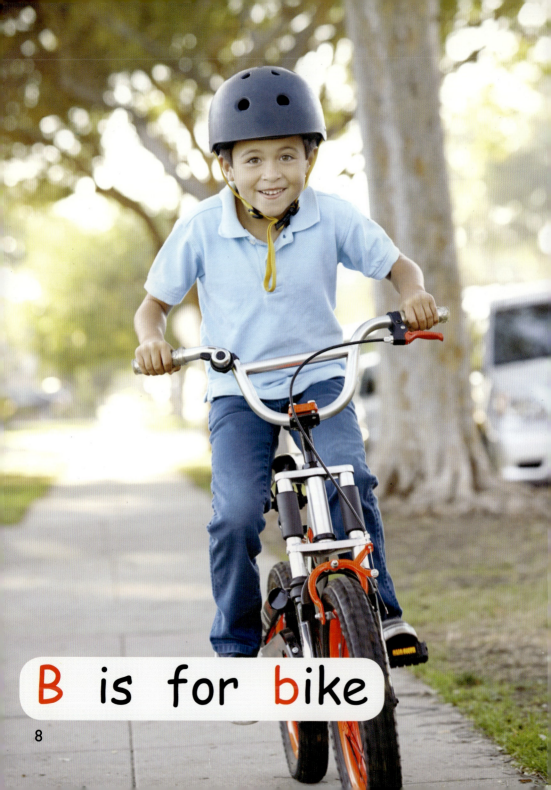

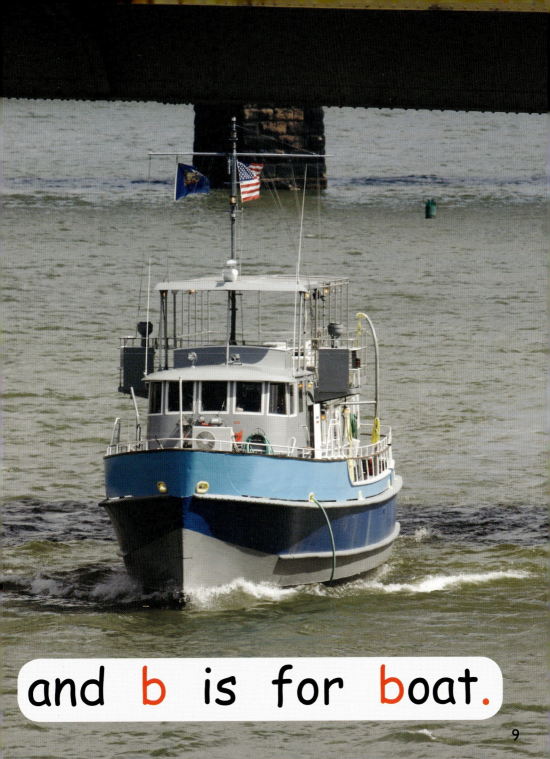

and b is for boat.

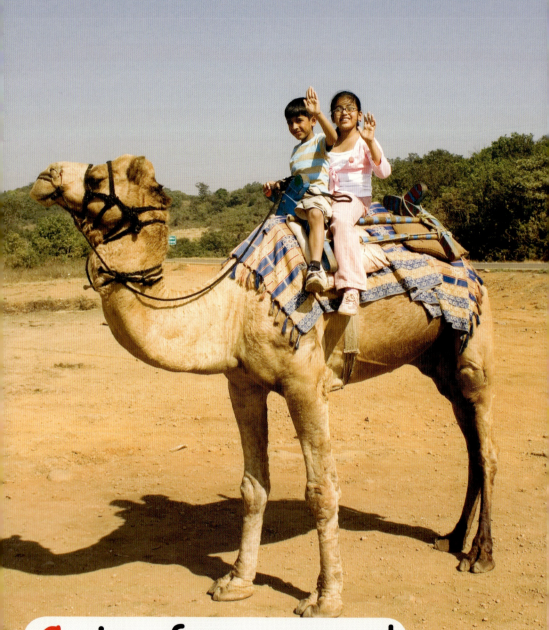

C is for camel

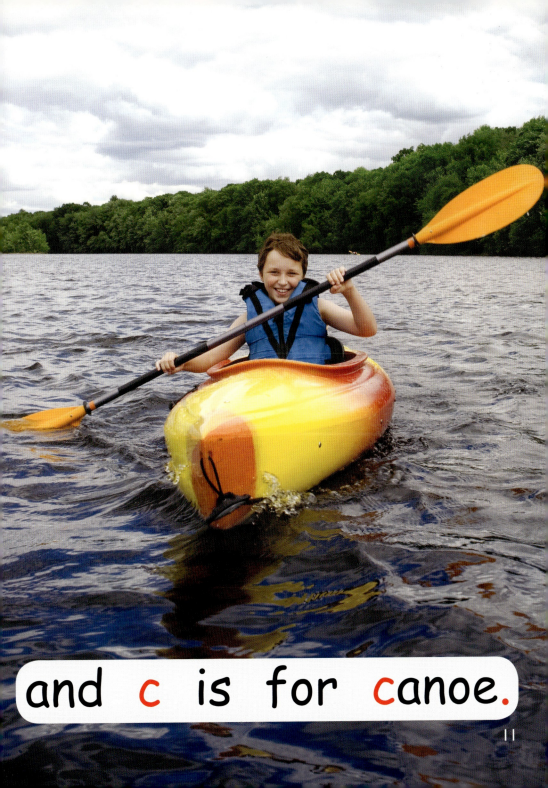

and c is for canoe.

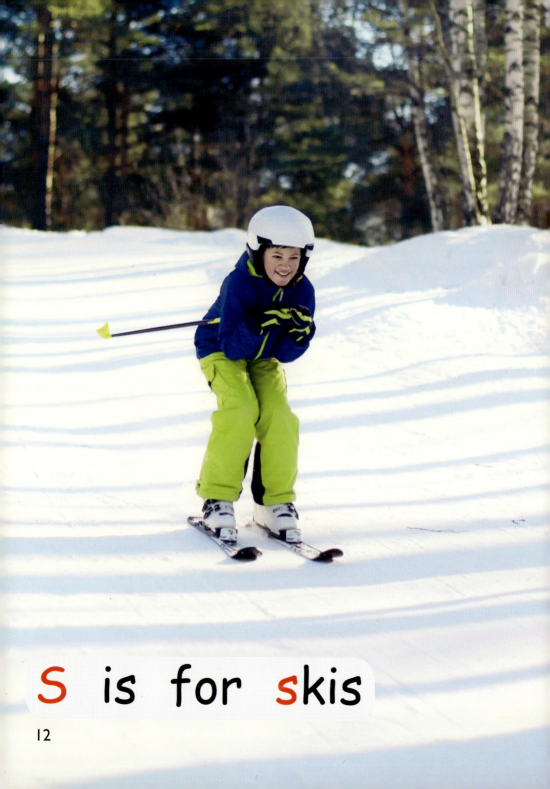

S is for skis

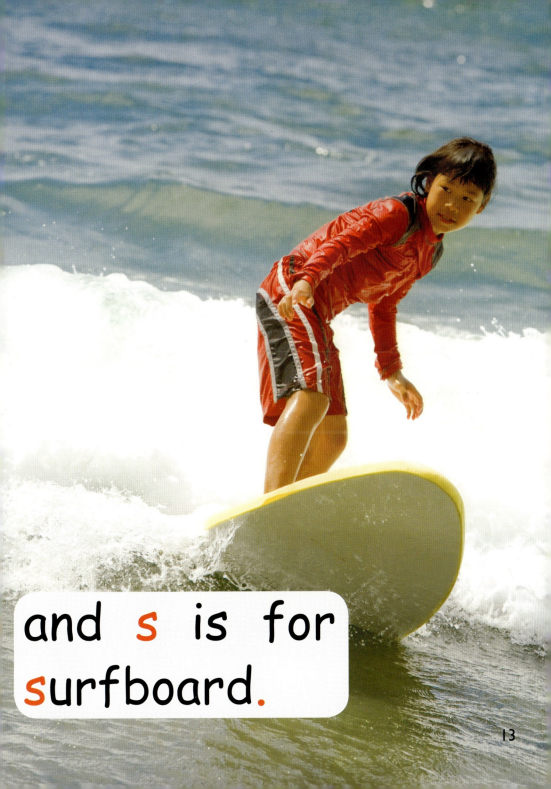

and s is for surfboard.

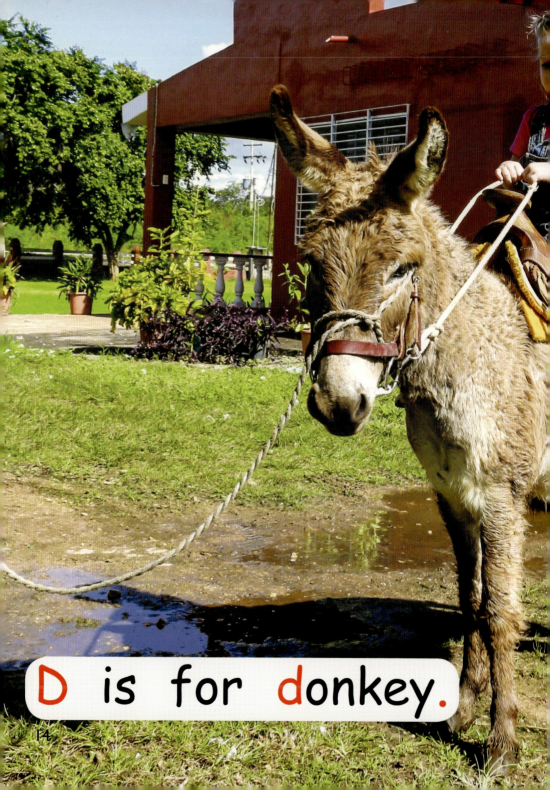
D is for donkey.

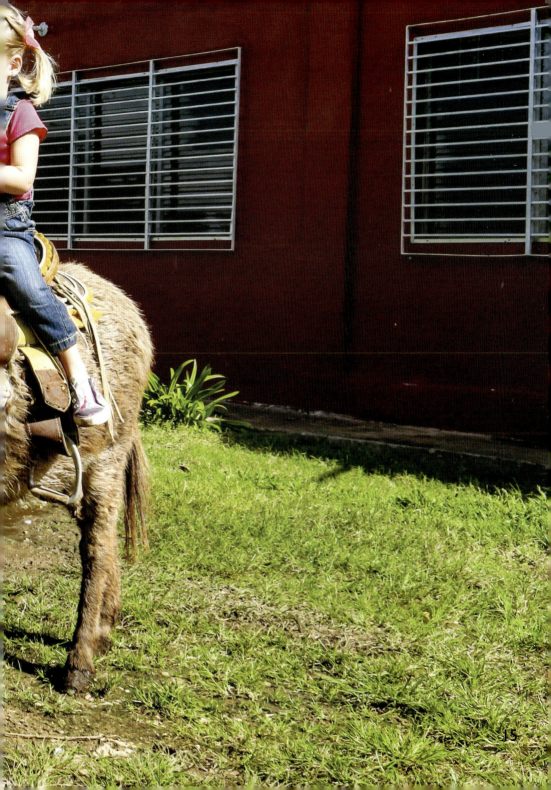

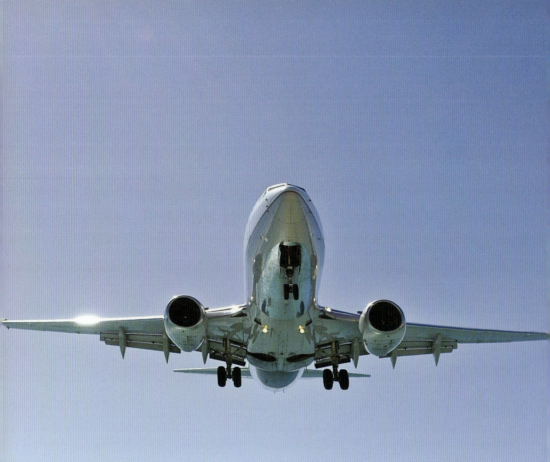

P is for plane.